DON'T STUFF UP YOUR PHYSICS EXAM.

Do this instead:

1) Buy this book.

2) Learn the 11 killer tips.

3) Sail through the exam.

4) Live happily ever after.

Tip 1:
Show Your Working

You mightn't believe this, but you can still get marks even when you <u>don't</u> get the answer right. If you show your <u>working</u> for calculations, the examiner can see that you were going along the <u>right lines</u>. Which is nice.

Tip 1 — Show Your Working

Write down every step

Don't just jump straight to the answer...

...Take it step by step and show your working.

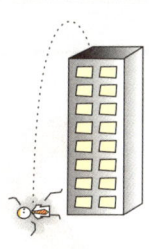

1) Quote the formula (if you're using one).

2) Make it clear when you're substituting in.

3) Write down the equation every time you rearrange it.

A buggy of mass 5 kg has kinetic energy of 90 J. Find the velocity of the buggy. *(3 marks)*

Kinetic energy, $KE = \tfrac{1}{2}mv^2$

Substituting in: $90 = \tfrac{1}{2} \times 5 \times v^2$

$90 = 2.5 \times v^2$

$36 = v^2$

Take square root: $v = 6 \text{ m/s}$

Even do it with simple calculations

Even with the simplest calculations you can press the wrong button.

Write the calculation you're about to do.

Do this with *every* practice question you do.

A wave has a time period of 0.05 s and a wavelength of 12 m. Calculate its velocity. *(4 marks)*

Frequency, $f = 1/T = 1/0.05 = 20 \text{ Hz}$

Velocity, $v = f \times \lambda = 20 \times 12 = 1.67 \text{ m/s}$ (to 3 s.f.)

D'oh — I hit divide instead of multiply, so the answer's *wrong*. But I still get 3 marks because my method was right.

If all else fails, make an educated guess

• If you're really not getting anywhere, don't leave it blank. Write down your best guess — it could be right.

• Don't spend too long on one question — if you're getting bogged down, guess at a calculation and then do it. You might get marks for any working that you've done.

Tip 2:
Use Formula Triangles

You've gotta learn the <u>formulas</u> for solving physics problems, or you'll throw away <u>easy marks</u>. With formula triangles you only need to <u>learn 1 formula</u>, and put it in a triangle to get <u>2 more</u> with no extra effort.

2 — Use Formula Triangles

Use formula triangles

1) If <u>2 letters are multiplied together</u> in the formula, they go on the <u>bottom</u> of the triangle. (Then the other letter goes on top.)

E.g. — $V = I \times R$ fits into the triangle like this:

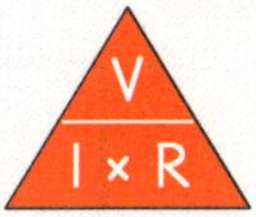

2) If <u>one thing's divided by another</u> in the formula then the one on top of the division goes <u>on top</u> in the triangle. (Then it doesn't matter which way round the other two go on the bottom.)

E.g. — $v = s / t$ fits into the triangle like this:

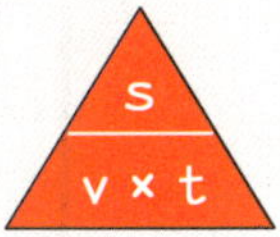

Remember to <u>use your thumb</u>...

1) Using formula triangles is super-easy. <u>Put your thumb over</u> the thing you want to find and write down what's left showing — this gives you your formula (so $I = V / R$).

2) Then put in the <u>values</u> for the other two things and <u>work out</u> the thing you don't know.

Use formula triangles even if there are more than three terms

1) Formula triangles still work when you've got more than 3 terms to deal with. Just put letters that are multiplied together on the bottom.

2) Practise rearranging each of your formulas so that you can put any of the values on the left-hand side.

Cover up height in the formula triangle and write out the rest.

Example:

A rocket of mass 240 kg is fired into the air and gains 28 kJ of gravitational potential energy. Calculate how high the rocket goes. (Take $g = 9.81$ N/kg.)

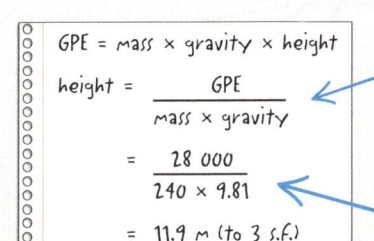

Then plug in the values.

Tip 3:
Get the Units Right

This one's so obvious it could get a degree in Obviousness from the University of St. Obvious: if you do a <u>calculation</u> and get the <u>units</u> right, you'll get <u>more marks</u> than if you get the units wrong or forget them completely. Obviously.

p 3 — Get the Units Right

Always include units in your answer

Physics calculations _always_ deal with real-life situations.
That means that the answers aren't just numbers — they _always_ need _units_.

> A car travels at 0.5 m/s for 4 seconds.
> What distance does it travel?
> Distance = speed × time   = 0.5 × 4   = 2

It could be 2 of anything, unless you put a unit afterwards.

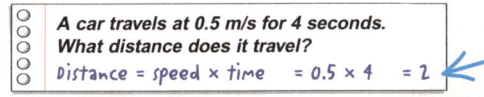

Learn those units

You want extra marks? Then learn the units, pal. Simple as that.

Potential difference	volts, V	Mass	kilograms, kg
Current	amps, A	Density	kg per m^3, kg/m^3
Resistance	ohms, Ω	Moment	newton-metres, Nm
Charge	coulombs, C	Speed/velocity	metres per sec, m/s
Power	watts, W	Acceleration	metres per sec^2, m/s^2
Energy	joules, J	Pressure	pascals, Pa (N/m^2)
Time	seconds, s	Area	$metres^2$, m^2
Force	newtons, N	Frequency	hertz, Hz
		Wavelength	metres, m

*types of energy (e.g. kinetic, potential) are measured in J. → Energy

Weight is a force too, so it's measured in N. → Force

Work out the units if you're not sure

Sometimes physicists don't have much of an imagination when they're naming units.
Some units are just _other units_ plonked together — so you can _work them out_ easily.

Examples:

Speed = distance / time

The starting units will be given in the question. → Distance in m, time in s
So Speed is measured in m/s

Density = mass / volume

Mass in kg, volume in m^3
So Density is measured in kg/m^3

Tricky unit to remember, but if you know the density formula then you're sorted.

If you're _really_ stuck, have a guess at the units
— e.g. if it's an energy question, chances are it's joules.

Tip 4:
Use Clever Memory Tricks

When you've got a whopping great <u>list</u> of things to learn, make up a <u>word</u> or <u>phrase</u> using the first letters. It'll help you remember the list and it means you can store 10,000 times as much info in your brain (NB: not true).

p 4 — Use Clever Memory Tricks

Use the memory tricks you've already got

1) Use memory tricks when you have to remember any list of things.
2) There are a few that you've probably seen already in class or in books. They come in two categories:

Words made from first letters ('acronyms')

e.g. Roygbiv

Sentences made from first letters ('mnemonics')

e.g. Richard Of York Gave Battle In Vain

Red, Orange, Yellow, Green, Blue, Indigo, Violet — both tricks help you remember the order of colours in the spectrum.

Make up your own

1) Start with a paragraph of your notes.

> There are four factors that affect the size of induced voltage in an electromagnet: the number of turns on the coil; the strength of the magnet; the area of the coil and the speed of movement.

2) Reduce the paragraph down to a few key words.

> Four factors affecting size of induced voltage in electromagnet:
> 1) Turns 2) Strength 3) Area 4) Speed

3) Then write out the first letter of each word in the list.

> T S A S
> S A T S

4) If there are a few vowels and it doesn't matter about the order of the list, try and rearrange the letters into a word. Then <u>remember</u> the word.

> Renewable energy resources:
> Wind; Waves; Tides; Hydroelectric; Solar; Geothermal; Food; Biomass
>
> W W T H S G F B
>
> **Why Would Tim Have Seven Gold Football Boots?**

5) If there are no vowels or if the order is important, make a sentence using the first letters.

6) Try and include one of your friends' names, and make it funny or rude (you'll remember it easier that way).

Tip 5:
Make Your Graphs Accurate

Plotting a graph is very much like admiring a beautiful... ahem... swan. Smooth <u>curved lines</u> and... um... plotted points marked with a <u>cross</u> could earn <u>extra marks</u>. OK, forget swans — if your graph looks duff, you'll <u>lose marks</u>.

5 — Make Your Graphs Accurate

Always plot and draw graphs carefully

This is what the examiner <u>doesn't</u> want to see:

Absolute pants

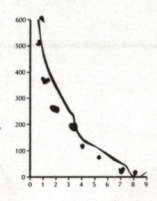

Even though the curve is more or less correct, you wouldn't get many marks because it's in a <u>total state</u>.

Example:

> Use the table to plot points on the grid below.
> Finish the graph by drawing the best curve.
> Use your graph to find the count rate after 2½ minutes. **(2 marks)**

Thickness of aluminium (mm)	1.0	2.0	3.0	4.0	5.0	6.0	7.0	8.0
Count rate (counts per minute)	600	300	144	72	36	18	0	0

1) Always use a pencil (a sharp one).

2) Plot the points by drawing crosses — they're much easier to read than splodges.

3) Do it accurately. The point should be marked by the <u>centre</u> of the cross.

4) If you're drawing a curve, make sure it <u>is</u> a curve. Make sure there are no straight bits and make it nice and smooth.

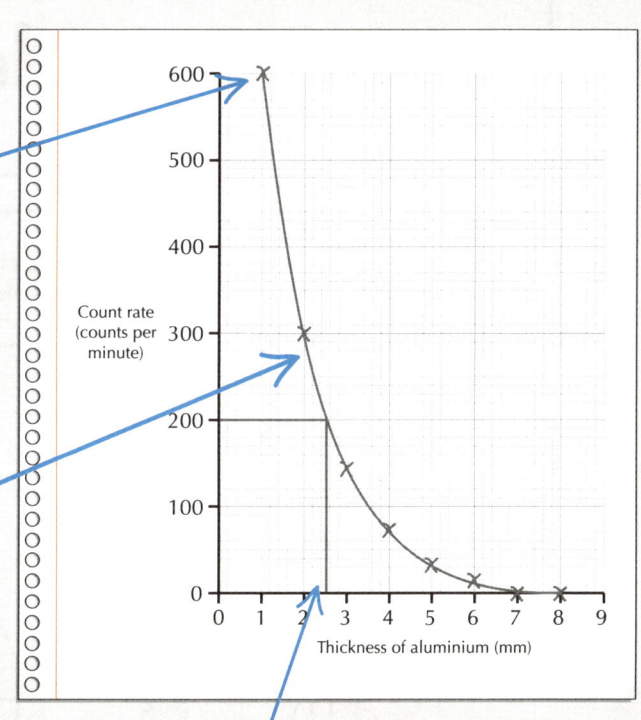

5) If you're told to read values off the graph, draw on the horizontal and vertical lines. It'll show the examiner that you used the graph and didn't just guess or work it out another way.

Tip 6: Get to Know Your Calculator

OK, I know, I know — OF COURSE you know how to use a calculator. But there's a world of difference between doing simple additions on a calculator and confidently working out <u>fractions</u>, using the <u>powers</u> button and storing answers in the <u>memory</u> (and retrieving them again).

Tip 6 — Get to Know Your Calculator

Sort out the basics first

1) Make sure you know how to use those buttons for calculations on your calculator.
2) For the ones you don't know, work out how to use them (find out from your teacher, your revision guide or whatever).
3) Write out how to do each one like this:

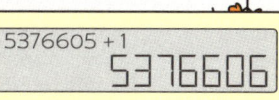

You should have <u>no problem at all</u> with using all the following buttons:

(goes without saying)

If you can't use brackets you'll make a lot of work for yourself.

> Brackets:
> Work out $\dfrac{3 \times (7+9)}{4-(8-6)}$:
> ③ ⊗ (⑦ ⊕ ⑨) ÷ (④ ⊖ (⑧ ⊖ ⑥)) =
> Answer should be 24.

Powers buttons save you having to keep pressing 'multiply'.

4) Practise loads and loads of calculations so you can do them with your eyes closed in the exam.

Fancier buttons make life easier...

These are the buttons that will save you loads of time in the exam.
If you've got time — figure out how to use them, write out the methods and learn them.

 The fraction button.

 The $\dfrac{1}{x}$ button.

 or The standard form button. (Saves you typing × 10 x^y 5.)

 For converting time to hours, minutes and seconds.

 or The 'add to memory' button. Use it to store bits of calculations until you need them...

 or MR ...then use the 'recall' button to bring them up again.

...but only use the ones you're sure about

1) If you're not totally sure how a button works — DON'T USE IT.
2) The exam is <u>not</u> the right place to figure it out.
3) If you haven't learnt it before you go in there, do calculations the long way and write out all your <u>working</u> (see Tip 1).
4) It's much safer to use methods you're used to. You <u>know</u> they work.

Tip 7:
Practise the 5 Big Question Types

Like Oasis songs, there are only a handful of <u>different types</u> of Physics questions. If you know exactly what they all <u>mean</u> then you won't have to spend vital exam time figuring out what you're actually being asked to <u>do</u>.

Top Tip 7 — Practise the 5 Big Question Types

Practise the five main types of question

There are a few types of exam questions that crop up again and again. Practise dealing with the key words, so you don't waste time in the exam.

1) **Calculate:**
   Pretty obvious really — get your calculator out.

   > A 600 kg car decelerates at 6.25 m/s². **Calculate** the braking force. *(1 mark)*
   > F = ma = 600 × 6.25 = 3750 N

2) **Write down:**
   Just short answers. Don't waste time writing loads.

   > **Write down** one factor other than mass that would affect a car's braking distance. *(1 mark)*
   > The speed of the vehicle.

3) **Describe:**
   Proper revision stuff — write down what you've learned from your notes.

   > **Describe** how increased mass affects the braking distance of a car. *(1 mark)*
   > With a larger mass, the car would take longer to stop.

4) **Suggest:**
   Like 'describe' questions — give one of the examples you've already learned.

   > **Suggest** one way that a car's braking distance could be reduced. *(1 mark)*
   > Carry fewer passengers in the car.

5) **Explain:**
   There are *two steps* here. First work out what's happening, then say what that *means*. (more people = more mass = greater braking distance)

   > **Explain** what would happen to the car's braking distance if it was full of people. *(2 marks)*
   > The overall mass of the car would be greater, so the braking distance would be greater.

Make sure you've done what the question asked

This might sound more obvious than a hedgehog hiding in a balloon, but...

1) If the question's asked for 3 facts, check you've *written* 3 facts.

2) If it tells you to explain your answer, check that you've answered the question *and* explained yourself.

3) If you're told to use a graph to calculate something, check that you've actually *used* it — even if you could have worked it out without the graph.

Tip 8:
Write the Right Amount

Not too much, not too little. If you write _less_ than the question's asking for, you definitely won't get all the _marks_. If you write _reams_ of stuff then you're just _wasting time_ that you could have spent on other questions. Or snoozing.

p 8 — Write the Right Amount

Work out how much you need to write

1) If it's a calculation question worth one mark, you need to show a bit of working. If it's worth 3 marks then include lots of working.

2) If it's a written question, check the <u>number of marks</u> so you do enough work, but not too much.

> One mark on offer — make <u>one</u> decent point.
> Two marks — <u>two</u> decent points.
> Three marks — <u>three</u> decent points.

(Can you see a pattern here?)

3) Another clue to how much to write is the number of lines they give you. If there's 10 lines, they're expecting 2 or 3 paragraphs, not a one-word answer.

Don't write too little... or too much

Here's a typical little exam question:

Describe and explain one use of ultrasound. (2 marks)

not enough

Kidney stones.

This probably won't even get you one mark. It doesn't describe what happens to kidney stones, let alone explain how ultrasound works. If it offers two marks, make two clear points.

Ultrasound is sound waves beyond the range of human hearing (i.e. frequencies above 20 kHz). It has loads of uses such as industrial cleaning. Ultrasound can be used to clean delicate mechanisms without them having to be dismantled, and is very effective at removing dirt on equipment. It can also break down kidney stones using high energy shockwaves to turn the stones into sand-like particles. In industrial quality control ultrasound waves can pass through something like a metal casting and whenever they reach a boundary between two different media (like metal and air) some of the wave is reflected back and detected. In pre-natal scanning of a foetus the ultrasound hits different media, some of the sound wave is reflected and these reflected waves are processed by computer to produce a video image of the foetus. Bats send out high-pitched squeaks (ultrasound) and pick up the reflections with their big ears. The same technique is used for sonar, which uses sound waves underwater to detect features in the water and on the seabed.

You've proved yourself a world expert on the subject. But that's just silly. Why bother?

You can only get two marks, max. So don't waste your precious exam time for no extra marks.

too much

Ultrasound beams can concentrate high energy shockwaves at kidney stones to turn them into sand-like particles, which can be passed out of the body.

Ahhh... Lovely. One use of ultrasound plus an explanation for two well-earned marks. And no time wasted.

Tip 9:
Make Sure Your Answer Isn't Ridiculous

It seems blummin' <u>obvious</u>, but if you just say "That's obvious, so I won't bother with it," you WILL slip up. What you need to do is make really sure you <u>check</u>, after every calculation, that your answer is not too <u>big</u>, too <u>small</u> or too <u>weird</u>.

Tip 9 — Make Sure Your Answer Isn't Ridiculous...

Your answers should make sense

1) Don't go thinking physics doesn't make sense. However bewildering what you learn may be, your answers to calculations have got to be sensible.
2) Check that:

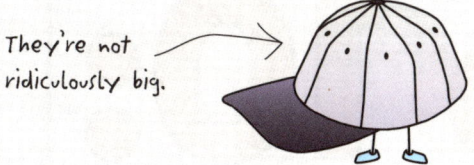
They're not ridiculously big.

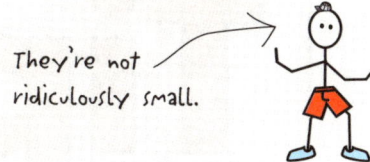
They're not ridiculously small.

After every question, check it's realistic

1) You don't have to know exact heights, weights or whatever.
2) Make sure it's vaguely reasonable. Normally if you make a mistake, it'll be a big one.

Examples:

	Calculate the speed of the bicycle.
O	0.02 ms^{-1} — nope (you'd fall off the bike).
O	82 ms^{-1} — you'd have to be Superman to go that fast.
O	3 ms^{-1} — sounds reasonable.

	How long would the kettle take to boil?
O	42 seconds — it's just possible, but sounds unlikely. Best check your answer to be sure.
O	26 minutes — no way.
O	3.5 minutes — feasible.

	Find the fuse rating for the hairdrier.
O	2.4 A — nope. Fuses come in 1, 3, 5 and 13 amp ratings.
O	5 A — that's more likely.

 — random

If you're stuck, try at random...
...and see if anything's reasonable

- If you're really stuck on a question and you've got 2 numbers, multiply them and divide each one by the other to get 3 numbers. Then see if it's obvious which one is right.
- Sometimes it's not obvious which one's right, but even so you can guess — and that's better than not writing anything down. But don't spend too long on it.
- This is a handy trick if you're stuck in the exam and really can't remember something... but don't use it as an excuse for not learning the formula in the first place.

Tip 10:
Get Circuit Diagrams Sussed

Time to put on my boring, preachy head for a couple of minutes...
Circuit diagrams aren't just there for decoration — they're <u>accurate diagrams</u> showing exactly how the circuit works. When you're <u>reading</u> circuit diagrams, the first thing is to decide if the circuit is in <u>series</u> or <u>parallel</u>. OK, rant over.

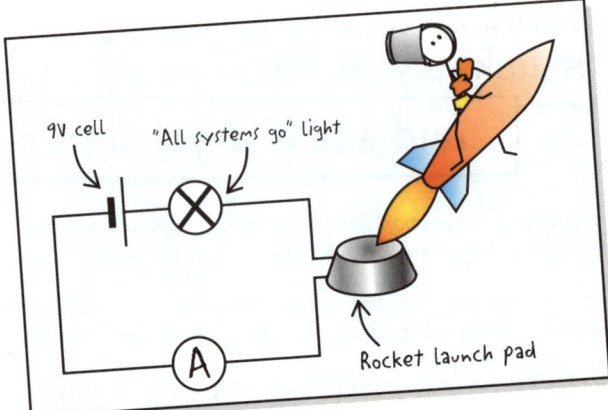

10 — Get Circuit Diagrams Sussed

Learn those circuit symbols

You won't get very far reading circuit diagrams if you don't know the symbols. These are all the ones you'll need — learn them <u>right now</u>.

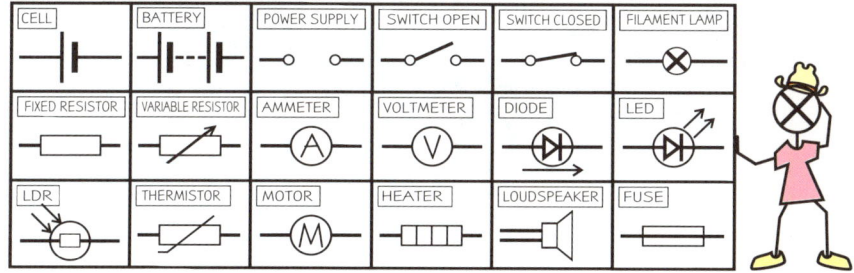

Figure out if the circuit is series or parallel

Exam questions often get you to work out what happens when switches are pressed or components are added to a circuit.

Series circuits (all the components in a line)

1) A switch in series turns the <u>whole</u> circuit <u>on</u> or <u>off</u>.

2) Adding another <u>bulb</u> in series means that <u>all</u> the bulbs go <u>dimmer</u>.

3) Adding another <u>cell</u> in series means that <u>all</u> the bulbs get <u>brighter</u>.

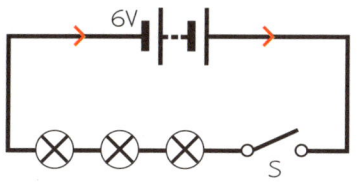

Parallel circuits (components in 'branches')

1) A switch on one of the 'branches' can <u>only</u> turn <u>that</u> branch on or off.

2) Adding another <u>bulb</u> in parallel <u>doesn't</u> affect bulb brightness at all...

3) ...and adding another <u>cell</u> in parallel <u>doesn't</u> affect bulb brightness either.

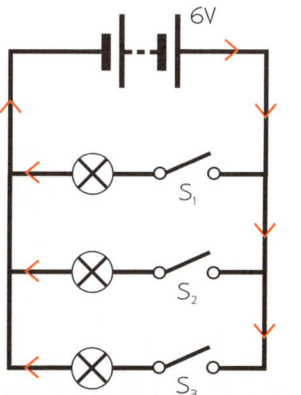

Tip 11:
Find Out What You Need To Know

Make sure that all your revision time is spent learning stuff you actually <u>need</u> for your exam. Each specification covers slightly <u>different</u> topics. You've got to learn <u>everything</u> that the exam board wants you to learn. Like, d'uh.

11 — Find Out What You Need To Know

Use your teacher

Don't just try and learn everything in the world about Physics.

Be crafty and learn what the exam board want you to learn.

1) Ask your teacher which specification you're doing. The big exam boards are OCR, Edexcel and AQA — it's probably one of those.

2) Pester your teacher for a copy of the specification, or a version they've made themselves. If your teacher puts up a fight, get hold of it yourself. The easiest way is on the Internet:

OCR:	www.ocr.org.uk
AQA:	www.aqa.org.uk
Edexcel:	www.edexcel.org.uk
Welsh:	www.wjec.co.uk
Irish:	www.ccea.org

Specification is just the faffy new name for syllabus.

Make yourself a checklist

1) Don't worry about all the rubbish at the beginning of the specification. The important bit is the content of the course you're doing.

2) Use the specification or your teacher's list to make a checklist of exactly what you need to know. Split the whole lot into topics and sub-topics.

3) Revise everything on the list, and don't bother revising anything else.

4) If you're using a course-specific CGP revision guide, then you can be sure that you need to know everything in the book and nothing more. Just use the contents page: section headings = topics; page titles = sub-topics.

5) If you're using a book that isn't course-specific, then cross out all the pages that don't apply to your specification.

Why not collect the lot?

Ask not what you can do for CGP, ask what CGP can do for you.

Revision Guides — £2*
Each revision guide covers an entire subject concisely without the waffle.

Workbooks  — £2*
Questions to test an entire subject. If the revision guide's shampoo, this is conditioner.

Practice Exam Papers — £1.25*
Full on exam practice with answers and mark schemes. Brown but beautiful.

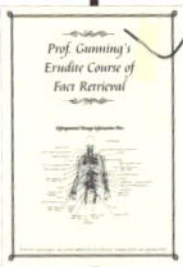

Prof. Gunning's Erudite course of Fact Retrieval — £1.15*
Tells you how to revise. Learn how to get shed-loads of facts into your head without heavy machinery.

Exam Tips — £1*
Subject specific exam tips. Sugar-coated exam-quenchers.

* small print — all money bits are school prices

TOTAL = £7.40 under eight squid

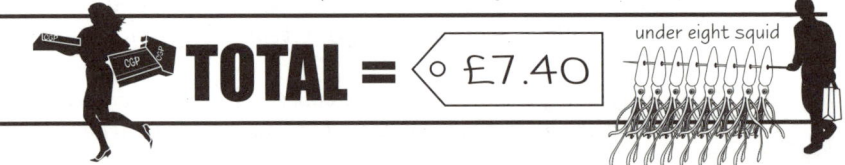

"My students love revising with me because we use CGP revision books."

Miss Roberts
English and Drama Teacher
Portsmouth

To order our books go to:

www.cgpbooks.co.uk

or phone 0870 750 1242